TASTE
OF THE
GAME

RECIPES INSPIRED BY *MAJOR LEAGUE BASEBALL*™

PHOTOGRAPHY BY ERIC WOLFINGER

Introduction 4

AMERICAN LEAGUE™ 6

AMERICAN LEAGUE EAST   DAVID ORTIZ 10

Dominican Tostones Sliders   NEW YORK YANKEES™ 12

Pit Beef Sandwiches   BALTIMORE ORIOLES™ 14

Grilled Boston Lobster Rolls   BOSTON RED SOX™ 16

Grilled Cuban Sandwiches   TAMPA BAY RAYS™ 18

Pulled Pork Poutine   TORONTO BLUE JAYS™ 20

AMERICAN LEAGUE CENTRAL   ERIC KARROS 24

Greek Lamb Burgers w/ Tzatziki Sauce   DETROIT TIGERS™ 26

Loaded Pork Sausage Sandwiches   CHICAGO WHITE SOX™ 28

'Cued Kielbasa Sandwich   CLEVELAND INDIANS™ 30

Saucy Buffalo Pig Wings   KANSAS CITY ROYALS™ 32

Grilled Walleye Sandwiches   MINNESOTA TWINS™...........34

AMERICAN LEAGUE WEST   VINNY CASTILLA 38

Tex-Mex Shrimp Cocktail   HOUSTON ASTROS™...............40

Barbecue Baked Potato
with Smoked Pork Shoulder   ANGELS™....................42

Original Nor-Cal BBQ Tri-Tip   OAKLAND ATHLETICS™.........44

Smoked Oysters w/ Spicy Miso Butter   SEATTLE MARINERS™ ...46

Bases Loaded Sandwiches:
Bacon, Baloney & Brisket   TEXAS RANGERS™ 48

EAST

CENTRAL

WEST

Contents

National League™ 52

   National League East OMAR VIZQUEL 56

Coal Fired Chicken Arepas MIAMI MARLINS™ 58

Grilled Tomahawk Pork Chops *w/ Peach Bourbon Glaze*

ATLANTA BRAVES™ 60

Filet Steak Sandwich NEW YORK METS™ 62

Burnt Ends Cheesesteak PHILADELPHIA PHILLIES™ 64

Grilled Chicken Souvlaki Skewers

   w/ Chopped Greek Salad WASHINGTON NATIONALS™ 66

   National League Central HAROLD REYNOLDS 70

St. Louis BBQ Ribs ST. LOUIS CARDINALS™ 72

Chicago-Style Char Dog CHICAGO CUBS™ 74

Grilled German Goetta Burgers CINCINNATI REDS™ 76

Beer & Cheese Sauced Brats MILWAUKEE BREWERS™ 78

Cheesesteak Burgers *w/ Fries & Coleslaw*

PITTSBURGH PIRATES™ 78

   National League West BYUNG-HYUN KIM 84

Spicy Korean-Style Chicken Wings LOS ANGELES DODGERS™ ... 86

Smoky Rattlesnake Chili ARIZONA DIAMONDBACKS™ 88

Grilled Rocky Mountain Oyster Po'Boy COLORADO ROCKIES™ . 90

Grilled Fish Tacos *w/ Smoky Lime Crema & Spicy Slaw*

SAN DIEGO PADRES™ 92

Grilled Vegetable Flatbreads *w/ Ricotta & Salsa Verde*

SAN FRANCISCO GIANTS™ 94

Index 96

EAST

CENTRAL

WEST

INTRODUCTION

Baseball and grilling adhere to a similar calendar, and rank high among the many reasons to look forward to the arrival of spring. And with each new spring, America's national pastime takes on an increasingly international flavor. A look at the 30 Major League Baseball rosters and inactive lists on Opening Day 2019 revealed the names of 251 players from 20 different countries and territories outside the 50 United States, according to MLB.com.

So baseball at its highest level, like the country of its origin, truly is a melting pot. Played from youth levels all the way to the top, it's a game rich with the universal language of sounds (the crack of the bat, the smack of the baseball in the catcher's mitt for Strike 3), sights (an outfielder using his glove to block the glare of the sun before using it to smother a high fly ball) and scents (rising in clouds of smoke from grills).

"Taste of the Game" is a tip of the cap to the myriad dishes that pair so well with baseball, a game with pastoral roots. True, baseball is as American as apple pie, but it's also as Caribbean as a Cubano sandwich, as Greek as a grilled lamb burger, as Canadian as pulled pork poutine.

We have included recipes from 30 different regions of North America for you to prepare while you're taking in a ballgame on the radio or television or just hanging out with friends and family.

Each of this book's six chapters opens with an accomplished baseball player tracing his personal grilling history to childhood. Our hope is that you take the flavors from "Taste of the Game" home with you, fire them up and savor them forever.

American
LEAGUE

"Making food for everyone, it's a way of connecting. That's what my mom did for all of us, and I learned from that."

DOMINICAN REPUBLIC

Big Papi has a motto: Go big, or go home. That applies to hitting.

And to serving as host.

When David Ortiz throws a party—and he loves to throw parties—he makes sure that he draws a crowd.

"I've never liked being alone," Ortiz says. "I want those big get-togethers, with 40 or 50 people around me: friends, neighbors, family. The kids are throwing the baseball around. There's music going and there's good stuff on the grill.

Everybody's eating and drinking and having a good time. That's my thing when I'm at home."

Ortiz owns several residences, but home for him always will be the Dominican Republic, where he was born and raised, and has a farm today. The sprawling property with pigs and chickens scattered here and there has a patio in back equipped with a grill. Big Papi is an equal-opportunity eater with a taste for poultry, pork and seafood. Every now and then, a vegetable sneaks in. But his favorite thing to fire over the coals is Brangus beef, a hybrid cross of Angus and Brahman cattle that Ortiz buys through a local broker. For seasoning, he sticks to salt and pepper.

"That meat is so tender and has so much flavor," Ortiz says. "I'm telling you, you don't need anything else."

Ortiz knows his way around a grill. But he says his skills can't compare to those of his beloved mother, Angela Rosa, who died in a car crash in 2002. Angela Rosa had what her son refers to as "that special touch," with everything she made. As a boy, Ortiz's long days playing baseball would give way in the evenings to happy gatherings around the family table.

"I was like the cleanup hitter," Ortiz says. "At the end of the night, nothing was ever left on my plate."

When he left home to pursue a baseball career, Ortiz missed those family meals. But he says he found good fellowship and good food in the company of other Dominican players. On road trips, they'd scout out Dominican restaurants or prepare dinner together in their hotel rooms.

"You know what it's like in those hotel kitchens," Ortiz says. "We'd be grilling a bunch of meat on one of those little stove tops. I was afraid we were going to burn the whole place down."

A festive slice of Caribbean culture can be found in clubhouses throughout the majors. Ortiz was one of many Dominican-born players who would show up on game days to share home-cooked meals with teammates. He says that some families were famous for

cooking up meals to share with players from both clubhouses, and fondly recalls one grilled dish that still makes his mouth water.

"Vladi's mom did this thing where she'd marinate the meat, then braise it, then finish it on the grill," Ortiz says. "I never asked exactly what she put in it, but her food was always one of the highlights of the season. I would look at the schedule and my stomach would start grumbling every time I saw we were going to Anaheim."

A larger-than-life figure on the diamond, Ortiz hasn't changed in retirement. He still enjoys being surrounded by good food and good company. His home-away-from-home these days is Miami, where he is building a new house with a modern kitchen and fully blown-out barbecuing station. The centerpiece is an expensive grill, with a giant flat-screen TV hanging overhead, far enough from the heat so as not to be a hazard but close enough so that Ortiz can watch a ballgame as he sears his favorite meats. On major holidays, he likes to make lechon, a traditional Caribbean roast pork dish.

"I'm just that kind of guy," Ortiz says. "I need people around me. Making food for everyone, it's a way of connecting. That's what my mom did for us, and I learned from that. So every time I'm around the grill, cooking something good, I feel like I'm hanging out with her."

For the Mojito Dip

¼	cup olive oil
¼	cup white vinegar
4	garlic cloves
½	teaspoon kosher salt

For the Tostones "Buns"

2	green plantains
2	cups canola or vegetable oil
3	teaspoons salt
8 ¼	inch sliced queso tropical

For the Cilantro Lime Aioli

½	cup mayonnaise
2	tablespoons fresh lime juice
2	garlic cloves
1	bunch cilantro, cleaned
	Kosher salt, to taste
	Ground black pepper, to taste

For the Sliders

8	2-ounce ground beef patties
1	tablespoon Goya Adobo Sazon
1	tablespoon garlic powder
8 ¼	inch sliced Dominican salami

DOMINICAN TOSTONES SLIDERS

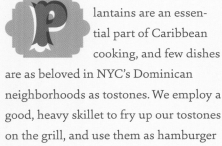

Plantains are an essential part of Caribbean cooking, and few dishes are as beloved in NYC's Dominican neighborhoods as tostones. We employ a good, heavy skillet to fry up our tostones on the grill, and use them as hamburger buns for these amazing beef sliders.

1. To make mojito dip, blend the oil, vinegar, garlic and salt. Set aside.

2. Using Kingsford® Charcoal, build a fire for direct grilling and preheat to 400 degrees Fahrenheit.

3. Make the slider "buns." Cut both ends from the plantains and remove skins. Slice into 1-inch pieces.

4. Add 3 teaspoons salt to a bowl of water and soak the plantains for at least 10 minutes.

5. Add oil to a heavy skillet and place on grill. Once hot, add plantains in batches, turning until golden brown on all sides. Remove from oil and drain on a paper towel-lined tray.

6. With a plate, flatten the fried plantains, and return to hot oil until golden brown and crispy. Use the same oil to fry the queso tropical, dropping the oil temperature to medium, and fry until golden brown, flipping as needed. Set aside to drain on paper towels.

7. Remove the plantains from the oil and toss with the mojito dip. Set aside.

8. To make cilantro lime aioli, place mayonnaise, lime juice, garlic and cilantro in a blender and puree. Salt and pepper to taste.

9. Season beef with sazon and garlic powder. Grill 5–8 minutes total, flipping once halfway through cooking. For your safety, please reference the USDA safe cooking temperatures. While the burgers are cooking, grill the salami until lightly charred, about one minute per side.

10. Place sliders onto fried tostones, top with 1 slice of salami and cheese, and 1 ounce cilantro aioli. Cover with another tostone and serve hot.

MAKES
6
sandwiches

PREP TIME
30
minutes + marinating time

COOK TIME
1
hour

3	tablespoons Kingsford™ Original All-Purpose Seasoning
2	pounds beef top round
½	cup sour cream
½	cup mayonnaise
½	cup prepared hot horseradish, drained

½	teaspoon kosher salt
¼	teaspoon freshly ground black pepper
6	hamburger buns or Kaiser rolls
1	sweet white onion, thinly sliced
2	ripe tomatoes, thinly sliced
	Iceberg lettuce (optional)

PIT BEEF SANDWICHES

Nothing says Baltimore tailgating like hot beef, sliced thin, sauced up, and piled high inside a Kaiser roll. It's called the pit beef sandwich, and it's been a Maryland street food favorite since the 1970s. Here's our fired-up take on this Baltimore barbecue classic.

1 Sprinkle rub all over the beef, patting it in. Place on a plate or in a baking dish, and cover with plastic wrap. You can let the rub marinate for a few hours, but for maximum flavor, leave it for 2 to 3 days in the refrigerator, turning once a day.

2 While the beef is marinating, mix together the sour cream, mayonnaise and horseradish in a small bowl. Season with 1/2 teaspoon salt and 1/4 teaspoon freshly ground black pepper. Refrigerate for at least a few hours.

3 Using Kingsford® Charcoal, build a fire for direct grilling and preheat to 400 degrees Fahrenheit. Oil the grill grates to prevent sticking.

4 Grill the beef 30 to 40 minutes, or until the outside has a nice bark, and is dark brown and the internal temperature reaches 120 degrees Fahrenheit (for rare). Turn the beef often. For your safety, please reference the USDA safe cooking temperatures.

5 Transfer to a cutting board; let it rest at least 10 minutes.

6 Slice the beef very thinly across the grain. Divide the beef and pile it onto the rolls.

7 Garnish each with the sliced onion and tomato (and the lettuce if using) and spoon on a few tablespoons of the horseradish sauce. Serve immediately.

GRILLED BOSTON LOBSTER ROLLS

ou might think of Maine when you hear "lobster roll," but proud Bostonians swear their version of this New England delicacy it tough to top. Be careful not to overcook that sweet, tender meat, or overwhelm it with salt and spices. Lobster should always be the star of the show.

1 Build a two-zone fire, placing preheated Kingsford® Charcoal briquets on one half of the bottom grill grate and leaving the other side void. Replace the top grill grate and adjust the bottom vents to bring the grill temperature to approximately 400 degrees Fahrenheit.

2 In a small bowl, combine 4 tablespoons butter, half of the herbs, Old Bay or similar seasoning, 1 teaspoon zest and 2 teaspoons lemon juice, and mix well. Set aside while you prepare the mayonnaise and lobster tails.

3 In a medium bowl, combine the celery, mayonnaise, remaining lemon juice and zest and herbs and cayenne pepper. Stir well and taste for seasoning. Set aside.

4 With a pair of heavy-duty kitchen shears, cut lengthwise down the center of the lobster tails' top shell to split the lobster meat in half. You can choose to split them completely or leave the bottom shell intact. Season with salt and pepper.

5 Place split lobster tails meat side down on the hot half of the grill. Grill the tails for approximately 2 minutes until the meat is lightly charred.

6 Flip tails over and grill for another 4–5 minutes while periodically basting with the seasoned butter. When done, the shell will have a bright red hue and the meat will be white.

7 If the lobster meat is still partially translucent, move to the cool side of the grill and cover until fully cooked.

8 When done, remove the lobster tails from the grill and let cool. For your safety, please reference the USDA safe cooking temperatures.

9 Brush the rolls all over with the remaining butter. Place rolls onto the grill, cut side down, for 2 minutes or until golden brown. Turn and brown the other sides.

10 Coarsely chop lobster meat and gently combine in the bowl with the mayonnaise mixture. Fill the toasted rolls with the lobster salad and serve immediately.

MAKES	PREP TIME	COOK TIME
4 sandwiches	**30** minutes	**10** minutes

6	tablespoons unsalted butter, melted and divided
2	tablespoons minced fresh herbs; parsley, tarragon, chives
1	teaspoon Old Bay or similar spice blend
2	teaspoons lemon zest
3	teaspoons fresh lemon juice
	Kosher salt, to taste
	Freshly ground black pepper, to taste
2	stalks celery, finely chopped
½	cup mayonnaise
	Pinch of cayenne or a few dashes of your favorite hot sauce
4	top-loading hot dog rolls
2	lobster tails, approximately 8 ounces each

RAYS

GRILLED CUBAN SANDWICHES

Although Floridians will always debate the Cuban Sandwich's birth city, nobody can deny the deliciousness of this culinary masterpiece. It became the lunch option of choice for Cuban cigar workers throughout Florida over a century ago, and was designated the Signature Sandwich of Tampa in 2012.

1 Cut the pork tenderloin in half crosswise to create two 4- to 5-inch-long pieces. Make a vertical cut down the middle of each piece, about 3/4 of the way through, opening the pieces like a book.

2 Lay pork pieces cut-side down on a piece of plastic wrap, cover with more plastic wrap and lightly pound the pork to about 1/2-inch thick with a meat mallet.

3 Add the pork, half the chopped garlic, lime and orange zest and juice, cumin, oregano, 3 tablespoons mustard, 3/4 teaspoon salt and 1/2 teaspoon pepper to a quart- or gallon-size resealable bag. Marinate the pork in the refrigerator for 30 minutes.

4 Using Kingsford® Charcoal, build a fire for direct grilling and preheat to 350 degrees Fahrenheit. Oil the grates to prevent sticking.

5 Transfer pork to a plate, shaking off excess marinade. Discard marinade. Grill until charred on both sides, 4 to 5 minutes per side for medium doneness. For your safety, please reference the USDA safe cooking temperatures.

6 Transfer the pork to a cutting board, and let rest for 5 minutes. Slice on slight angle into 1/8-inch-thick slices.

7 In a small bowl, combine the remaining chopped garlic and 3 tablespoons mustard with mayonnaise and whisk together. Slice the ciabatta or rolls in half horizontally and spread the mayo mixture on both sides of the bread.

8 Place a slice of Swiss cheese on each bottom section and top with 3 to 4 slices of the pork tenderloin, 3 to 4 pickle slices, 2 slices of ham, 3 slices of salami, a second slice of Swiss cheese, and the top half of the roll. Wrap

sandwiches in a double layer of aluminum foil.

9 Place foil-wrapped sandwiches on the grill and place a cast iron skillet or brick on top of each sandwich. Grill about three minutes per side while pressing down on the skillet or brick, until the cheese has melted and the bread is browned and crunchy.

10 Unwrap sandwiches, cut in half, and serve immediately.

MAKES	PREP TIME	COOK TIME
4 sandwiches	**20** minutes	**16** minutes

1	pound pork tenderloin
4	cloves garlic, finely chopped, divided
1	lime, zested and juiced
1	small orange, zested and juiced
1	teaspoon ground cumin
1	teaspoon dried oregano
6	tablespoons Dijon mustard, divided
¾	teaspoon salt
½	teaspoon pepper
¾	cup mayonnaise
4	small ciabatta loaves or Kaiser rolls
8	thin slices Swiss cheese
1	cup bread and butter pickle slices
8	thin slices deli ham
12	slices of Genoa salami

MAKES
4
servings

PREP TIME
45
minutes

COOK TIME
10
hours

For the pork dry rub

2	tablespoons dark brown sugar
¼	cup white sugar
¼	cup paprika
3	tablespoons garlic salt
3	tablespoons kosher salt
1 ½	teaspoons chili powder
½	teaspoon dried oregano
¼	teaspoon cayenne pepper
½	teaspoon cumin
½	teaspoon black pepper

For the pork injection

⅓	cup apple juice
¼	cup water
¼	cup sugar
2	tablespoons kosher salt
1	tablespoon Worcestershire sauce

For the pork

1	7-pound pork shoulder
¾	cup KC Masterpiece® Original Barbecue Sauce
2	pounds frozen crinkle cut french fries
	Kosher salt, to taste
¾	cup cheese curds

ries. Cheese. Gravy. What's not to love? If you're not familiar with the Canadian creation of poutine, it's time to make up for lost time. Our version features tender pulled pork smoked on the grill, with just the right touch of KC Masterpiece® Barbecue Sauce.

1. Prepare charcoals using the snake configuration, and add soaked Kingsford™ Wood Chips along the line of coals. Place a foil pan with hot water in the center of the snake.

2. Light about eight briquets in a chimney. When ready, pile all of the lit coals at the head of the charcoal snake. The coals will burn down slowly as the meat cooks.

3. Inject pork shoulder evenly with solution. Apply a generous amount of dry rub onto the meat.

4. Place pork shoulder fat side up on the rack, cover, and bring the grill temperature up to a constant 225 to 250 degrees Fahrenheit, using the vents to regulate heat.

5. Check the temperature of the grill every hour, adding more charcoal and soaked wood chips as needed to maintain heat.

6. Smoke for about 8–9 hours or until the internal temperature of the pork

PULLED PORK POUTINE

reaches about 205 degrees Fahrenheit.

7. Paint the shoulder with half of the barbecue sauce in the last 20 minutes of cooking. Carefully remove and let rest for at least 15 minutes before shredding into large chunks.

8. Make the french fries according to package directions. If they are not seasoned well enough, add a little bit of salt when they come out of the oven.

9. To make the poutine, use a double thick layer of aluminum foil, and bend it up on the sides to create a large boat. Pile the fries inside and top with the cheese curds. Mix 1 pound of pulled pork with the remaining sauce, and add to the poutine.

10. Place the whole thing on the grill just until warmed through and the cheese is melted. Serve immediately.

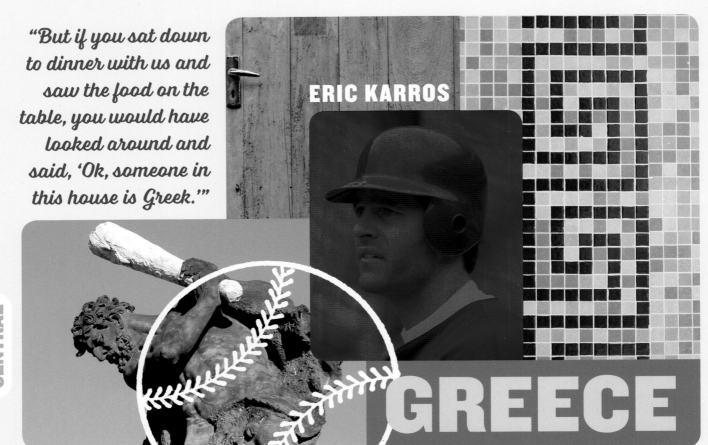

> "But if you sat down to dinner with us and saw the food on the table, you would have looked around and said, 'Ok, someone in this house is Greek.'"

ERIC KARROS

GREECE

A look at the Los Angeles Dodgers long list of Rookie of the Year winners illustrates what a melting pot baseball has become. A record 18 Dodgers have won the award, which is twice as many as any other organization.

The winners were born in the Dominican Republic, Japan, Mexico and the United States of Alabama, Arizona, California, Georgia, Michigan, Missouri, North Carolina, New Jersey, Ohio, Pennsylvania and Tennessee.

Baseball's first winner of the award was more famous for breaking baseball's color barrier and was the first of four African-American Dodgers named Rookie of the Year in a seven-year span.

Eric Karros was National League ROY in 1992, triggering a run of five consecutive Dodgers to garner the award.

All it takes to trace the roots of his ancestors is a peek at what's on his grill on a typical sun-splashed Los Angeles day: seared lamb chops and chicken, seasoned with oregano and lemon, a nod to the Greek cooking he enjoyed as a child.

"It's not like everyone in my family hung out dancing and spinning plates in the kitchen every night, like 'My Big Fat Greek Wedding,'" Karros says, referencing the 2002 film. "But if you sat down to dinner with us and saw the food on the table, you would have looked around and said, 'OK, someone in this house is Greek.'"

That someone was Karros' father, George, whose own father, Panayotis, left Greece as a teenager, in 1916, searching for a better life. His entry point to the United States was Ellis Island, where his last name was shortened. Karacassonis became Karros. For Panayotis, the name change was a step toward assimilation. Baseball became that for his son.

"My dad's name is George Aristotle Karros," Karros says. "But he was born in this country and he was totally in love with baseball from the start. It was a big part of his identity as an American. He was the child of immigrants, and when I think back on it, I realize, baseball was kind of his way in."

When Eric was a boy, Vin Scully's voice spoke to father and son as they bonded over baseball listening to Dodgers games on the radio in George's office. When they went to the ballpark, they both enjoyed grilled Dodger Dogs.

The meals at home weren't nearly as predictable. Karros' mother was of Swedish and Scottish descent, but also developed

a deft hand with Greek dishes, from grilled whole fish to garlicky lamb meatballs.

"There wasn't much she didn't know how to make," Karros says. "It seemed like every night was something new."

Family trips to New York to visit relatives gave rise to even more elaborate feasts, with Greek cousins, aunts and uncles gathered around the table. Karros was living well, but it wasn't until he left home that he realized just how good he had it. Cooking for himself on a portable grill, he did his best to replicate the dishes of his youth. He came to learn that the key was to take the same approach that he took to hitting: stick to the fundamentals.

"Olive, lemon, oregano, salt," Karros says. "You can't really go too wrong with those."

His grill behind his home, flanked by granite, has a bar around it and speakers above it. He and his wife routinely have their children's Little League teams over for dinner. Karros doesn't claim to be the world-class cook that he considers his mom to be, but he has the skill to please a crowd, whether he's grilling lemony Greek dishes or hot dogs and hamburgers, all classically American cookouts.

"The point is to just get everyone together and have a good time," Karros says. "To me, that's what it's all about."

GREEK LAMB BURGERS with Tzatziki Sauce

DETROIT TIGERS™ | AMERICAN LEAGUE™ CENTRAL

MAKES	PREP TIME	COOK TIME
4 sandwiches	**30** minutes	**10** minutes

½ English (hothouse) cucumber, peeled, seeds removed

1 garlic clove, minced

1 cup plain Greek yogurt

¼ cup fresh mint leaves, finely chopped, divided

2 tablespoons extra-virgin olive oil

Kosher salt and ground black pepper, to taste

¼ cup crumbled feta cheese

¼ cup Kalamata olives, pitted and chopped

¼ cup finely chopped red onion

1 tablespoon fresh oregano leaves, finely chopped

1 pound ground lamb

4 small round Greek-style pita breads (4 to 6-inch)

½ small head iceberg lettuce, shredded

2 Roma tomatoes, thinly sliced

IN the great city of Detroit, just a stone's throw away from the stadium, you'll find Greektown, a historic neighborhood with some of the best eats in Michigan. This hearty pita burger features a Greek-inspired combination of savory lamb and creamy tzatziki sauce.

1 To make the tzatziki sauce, shred the cucumber on the coarse side of a box grater. Place in a sieve or thin kitchen towel and squeeze the liquids out to drain. Place in a small bowl. Add the minced garlic, Greek yogurt, half of the chopped mint, and olive oil and blend well. Season with salt and pepper, to taste. Cover and refrigerate for about an hour before serving.

2 In a medium bowl, combine feta, olives, onion, oregano, remaining mint, 1 teaspoon salt and ½ teaspoon pepper. Add lamb and mix lightly with your hands, taking care not to overwork.

3 Form into 4 patties of even thickness. Transfer to a plate, cover loosely with plastic wrap and refrigerate for 30 minutes.

4 Meanwhile, prepare the grill. Using Kingsford® Charcoal, build a fire for direct grilling and preheat to 400 degrees Fahrenheit.

5 Cook the burgers, flipping once, until cooked to your desired doneness, about 5 minutes per side for medium. For your safety, please reference the USDA safe cooking temperatures.

6 When done, set burgers aside to rest for a few minutes..

7 Serve the lamb burgers folded inside the pita bread with plenty of lettuce, a few slices of tomato and tzatziki sauce on top.

LOADED PORK SAUSAGE SANDWICHES

MAKES	PREP TIME	COOK TIME
6 sandwiches	**15** minutes	**40** minutes

2 green bell peppers, stemmed and seeded

1 red bell pepper, stemmed and seeded

3 tablespoons olive oil, plus more for brushing

2 pounds Italian sausages, hot or mild

1 yellow onion, sliced

2 garlic cloves, minced

½ pound button mushrooms, sliced

1 15-ounce can diced tomatoes

2 teaspoons dried Italian herb blend

1 tablespoon balsamic vinegar

½ teaspoon salt

¼ teaspoon pepper

6 hero or hard rolls, each about 6 to 8 inches long, split

¼ cup freshly grated Parmesan cheese (optional)

C hicagoans love a loaded sausage sandwich, and this fired up ballpark beast is a beauty. It's a grilled pork sausage nestled in a hardy roll, piled high with sautéed veggies, and topped with cool tomatoes.

1 Build a charcoal fire for direct grilling using Kingsford® Charcoal and preheat to 400 degrees Fahrenheit.

2 Cut the peppers into quarters and brush them with some olive oil. Place the peppers on the grill, skin side down, for about 15 minutes until the skins are charred black.

3 Place the peppers in a bowl and cover with plastic wrap until they are cool enough to handle, about 10 minutes. Wipe away the charred skin from the peppers with paper towels, cut into thin strips and set aside.

4 Place the sausages on the grill and cook for around 15 minutes, turning the sausages throughout the cooking process. For your safety, please reference the USDA safe cooking temperatures. Set aside on a cutting board to rest.

5 Meanwhile, heat a large frying pan over

medium-high heat. Add the 3 tablespoons olive oil and sauté the onions, garlic and mushrooms for 4 to 5 minutes.

6 Add the tomatoes, herbs, balsamic vinegar, and 1/2 teaspoon salt and 1/4 teaspoon pepper. Bring to a boil, lower to a simmer and stir in the sliced peppers. Heat through for a few more minutes.

7 Prepare the rolls by brushing cut sides with oil and grill (cut sides down) until the bread is lightly toasted. Cut the rested sausages diagonally into 3/4-inch thick slices and divide among the toasted rolls.

8 Top with the tomato-pepper mixture. Garnish with a sprinkling of Parmesan and serve.

'CUED KIELBASA SANDWICH

Cleveland is the proud home of the Polish Boy, a kielbasa sausage nestled in a bun and topped with slaw, BBQ sauce and fries. We call our version the 'Cued Kielbasa Sandwich. It's a magnificent meal in a bun, and it's always ready for game day.

1 To make the coleslaw, place the cabbage, onions and jalapeño in a bowl. In a smaller bowl, mix the apple cider vinegar, mustard, mayonnaise and sugar together. Toss with the cabbage mixture until evenly coated. Season to taste with salt and pepper and set aside.

2 Make the french fries according to package directions. If they are not seasoned well enough, add a little bit of salt when they come out of the oven.

3 Using Kingsford® Charcoal, build a charcoal fire for direct grilling and preheat to 400 degrees Fahrenheit.

4 Butterfly kielbasa by slicing them lengthwise without cutting all the way through. Open gently so they lay flat on the grill.

5 Cook for about 5 minutes on each side, until charred in spots and hot throughout. For your safety, please reference the USDA safe cooking temperatures.

6 To build the sandwiches, place a kielbasa inside each roll, top with plenty of coleslaw and french fries, and drizzle with barbecue sauce. Serve immediately.

MAKES	PREP TIME	COOK TIME
4 servings	**20** minutes	**20** minutes

3	cups green cabbage, shredded
½	small onion, julienned
½	jalapeño, minced
2	tablespoons apple cider vinegar
1	tablespoon brown mustard
2	tablespoons mayonnaise
1	teaspoon sugar
	Kosher salt and ground black pepper, to taste
2	pound bag frozen straight-cut french fries
4	kielbasa sausages
4	hoagie buns or other long sandwich rolls
½	cup KC Masterpiece® Original Barbecue Sauce

KANSAS CITY ROYALS™ | AMERICAN LEAGUE™ | CENTRAL

SAUCY BUFFALO PIG WINGS

Pig wings, for the uninitiated, are small pork shanks that have been "French trimmed," exposing the bone to leave a chunk of meat at one end. They're a heftier alternative to chicken wings and grill up fast, perfect for a pre-game feast.

1 Using Kingsford® Charcoal, build a fire for direct grilling and preheat to 400 degrees Fahrenheit.

2 Season the pig wings on all sides with the garlic, celery salt, kosher salt and pepper to taste. Rub in olive oil to coat evenly.

3 Place the wings on the grill and cook, turning often, until slightly charred and cooked through, about 15 minutes. For your safety, please reference the USDA safe cooking temperatures.

4 While the wings are cooking, stir the hot sauce together with the melted butter and the vinegar. Baste the wings and continue to cook, turning and basting occasionally, for another five minutes, until the wings are glazed and golden. Discard hot sauce after basting.

5 Serve hot, with blue cheese dressing and celery on the side, if desired.

MAKES	PREP TIME	COOK TIME
6	**15**	**20**
servings	minutes	minutes

4	pounds pig wings
2	teaspoons granulated garlic
2	teaspoons celery salt
	Kosher salt, to taste
	Ground black pepper, to taste
3	tablespoons olive oil
1	cup Frank's RedHot Original sauce
4	tablespoons unsalted butter, melted
2	teaspoons white vinegar
	Celery, for serving
	Blue cheese dressing, for serving

GRILLED WALLEYE SANDWICHES

T he icy waters of Minnesota are home to some of the most coveted freshwater fish in the country, so it's no wonder that the Twin Cities are known for their walleye sandwiches. Of course, our version is flame grilled, to let those fresh-caught flavors shine.

1 To make the tartar sauce, whisk the mayonnaise, chopped dill pickle, 1 teaspoon lemon zest, 1 tablespoon lemon juice, Dijon mustard, 1 tablespoon fresh or 1 teaspoon dried dill, half of the garlic, and 1 tablespoon olive oil in a small bowl until smooth.

2 Season with 1/2 teaspoon salt and 1/4 teaspoon pepper. Cover and refrigerate until ready to use.

3 Using Kingsford® Charcoal, prepare the grill for direct cooking and preheat to 350 degrees Fahrenheit.

4 In a small bowl, combine the remaining lemon zest and juice, dill, garlic and olive oil. Add hot sauce to taste. Set aside.

5 Season the fish fillets on both sides with salt and pepper.

6 Grease the grill grates and place directly over the prepared medium coals. Slightly overlap the lemon slices on the grill grates in a pattern to accommodate the fish fillets.

7 Place the fish directly on the lemon slices. Brush with the lemon-dill mixture. Cover the grill and cook for 10 to 12 minutes or until fish flakes easily when tested with a fork. Don't turn the fish. For your safety, please reference the USDA safe cooking temperatures.

8 To assemble, lightly toast and butter the rolls. Spread the tartar sauce on both sides of each roll and place one fish fillet into each roll.

9 Top with pickle slices, shredded lettuce and tomato. Serve immediately.

MAKES	PREP TIME	COOK TIME
4	**20**	**15**
sandwiches	minutes	minutes

½	cup mayonnaise
2	tablespoons finely chopped dill pickle
2	teaspoons grated lemon zest, divided
3	tablespoons lemon juice, divided
1	teaspoon Dijon mustard
2	tablespoons snipped fresh dill or 2 teaspoons dried dill, divided
4	cloves garlic, minced, divided
3	tablespoons olive oil, divided
½	teaspoon kosher salt
¼	freshly ground black pepper
4	boneless, skinless walleye fillets (about 1½ pounds)
	Hot sauce of choice, to taste
3	or 4 lemons, thinly sliced
4	soft sub or hot dog rolls
1	cup dill pickle slices
2	cups shredded iceberg or romaine lettuce
2	tomatoes, sliced 1/4-inch thick

VINNY CASTILLA

For Vinny Castilla, there was nothing like Mom's cooking. Except maybe Dad's cooking.

MEXICO

VISITANTES 4 0 1 3 0 1 1 0 1

Tiburones DE HOLBOX 1 0 1 2 0 1 1 3

The aromas and tastes from his youth in Oaxaca, Mexico return for Vinny Castilla when he thinks back to the days of his mother, Maria, hand-pressing fresh tortillas, simmering black beans, and making room on the plates for empanadas, quesadillas and memelas, those delectable corn cakes.

The middle child of three, Vinny would have no reason ever to suspect that any meal could rival his mother's. And then his father, Carlos, fired up the grill, a brick-and-stone foundation topped with a metal grate, with room underneath for charcoal.

A school teacher, Carlos would get the embers of the front-yard grill glowing and the good grub going on weekends.

He could grill flavor into chicken, but that wasn't his calling card. He specialized in carne asada, a classic dish of seared, sliced beef. Chefs all have their own versions of carne asada, the seasonings and cuts ranging widely, from skirt steak rubbed with crushed garlic and cilantro to flank steak marinated in chiles, lime and beer.

Carlos kept his version as simple as his son's powerful, see-the-ball-crush-it-over-the-fence swing. A three-time Silver Slugger winner at third base and a two-time All-Star, Vinny belted 320 home runs in 16 seasons, nine spent with the Colorado Rockies. Vinny hit 320 home runs in his career, a big number, except when compared to the number of times his father smashed it out of the park on his grill.

Carlos' secret: He bought the best beef he could find, sprinkled it with salt and set it on the grill for a just-so char. Maria prepared the only extras: fresh salsas, guacamole and warm tortillas.

"I'm telling you, it all was so good," Vinny says. "You didn't need anything else."

He spent his childhood in Oaxaca—then a fast-growing city with a small-town feel—mostly outdoors, riding bikes and playing baseball in a neighborhood brimming with children. Vinny remembers it as a town where folks left their front doors open. It was understood that when food was on the table, it was everyone's to share.

Playing baseball kindled his appetite for eating the grilled treasures, as did watching his favorite sport on TV every fifth day. The local station would broadcast Dodgers games when a certain young phenom from Etchohuaquila, Mexico was the starting pitcher

While watching the left-hander with the high leg kick roll his eyes to the sky in mid-delivery, the Castillas feasted on mom's shrimp cocktail, salsa and guacamole to complement dad's grilled carne asada. Always prepared for big turnouts, dad chopped the meat for use in tacos so the supplies wouldn't run dry.

"I had a very happy childhood," Vinny says. "Playing baseball was a big part of that, but so was the feeling in my house. We didn't have a lot of money, but we had a lot of warmth and love and good food. If you came over, and the baseball game was on, you knew you were going to be well fed."

Before Castilla left home, his dad taught him some basic grilling

skills, enough so that he could make a steak sizzle. But it wasn't until Vinny settled down with wife, Samantha, and their three children that the torch fully passed from father to son. Outside of his Colorado home, Castilla has installed an ample grill. He uses it as often as the weather allows, usually starting around Spring Training and keeping it firing well into autumn.

Vinny can grill tasty chicken, but as with his father, his specialty is beefier: skirt steak, flank steak, rib-eye, hanger, all seasoned with the simplicity favored by Carlos: rubbing it with salt and nothing else for just the right char. Following a recipe learned from mother-in-law Maria, Samantha creates a fiery serrano chile salsa. Then they gather around the table with family and friends, often with the sights and sounds of a ballgame showing on TV as all the musical background they need.

"The food is really good," Castilla says. "But it's more than that. It feels like we're keeping a tradition alive."

TEX-MEX SHRIMP COCKTAIL

MAKES	PREP TIME	COOK TIME
4-6 skewers	**20** minutes	**6** minutes

½ cup ketchup

¼ cup lime juice

1 cup pico de gallo

2 tablespoons Cholula® hot sauce,
    plus more to taste

¼ cup olive oil

1 avocado, diced

Kosher salt and ground black
    pepper, to taste

2 pounds jumbo Gulf shrimp,
    peeled, deveined, tails left on

1 tablespoon vegetable oil

2 tablespoons chopped fresh
    parsley or cilantro leaves

Metal or wooden skewers
    (soaked in water for about 30
    minutes)

When the summer sun hits, hungry Texans reach for the brighter, lighter flavors of Tex-Mex cuisine. This hearty shrimp cocktail is an explosion of tangy citrus, creamy avocado, savory spices and sweet, Texas-sized Gulf shrimp.

1 To make the sauce, whisk together the ketchup, lime juice, pico de gallo, hot sauce and olive oil. Gently stir in the avocado, season to taste with salt and pepper, and set aside. Add more hot sauce if desired.

2 Using Kingsford® Charcoal, prepare the grill for direct cooking and preheat to 450 degrees Fahrenheit.

3 Place shrimp in a large bowl, add the vegetable oil and season with salt and pepper, to taste. Toss well to combine.

4 Thread seasoned shrimp onto the skewers. Gently place the shrimp skewers on the grill. Cook for 2 to 3 minutes total per side. The shrimp is ready when bright pink and slightly charred. For your safety, please reference the USDA safe cooking temperatures.

5 Serve the shrimp with the Mexican cocktail sauce, garnished with chopped cilantro.

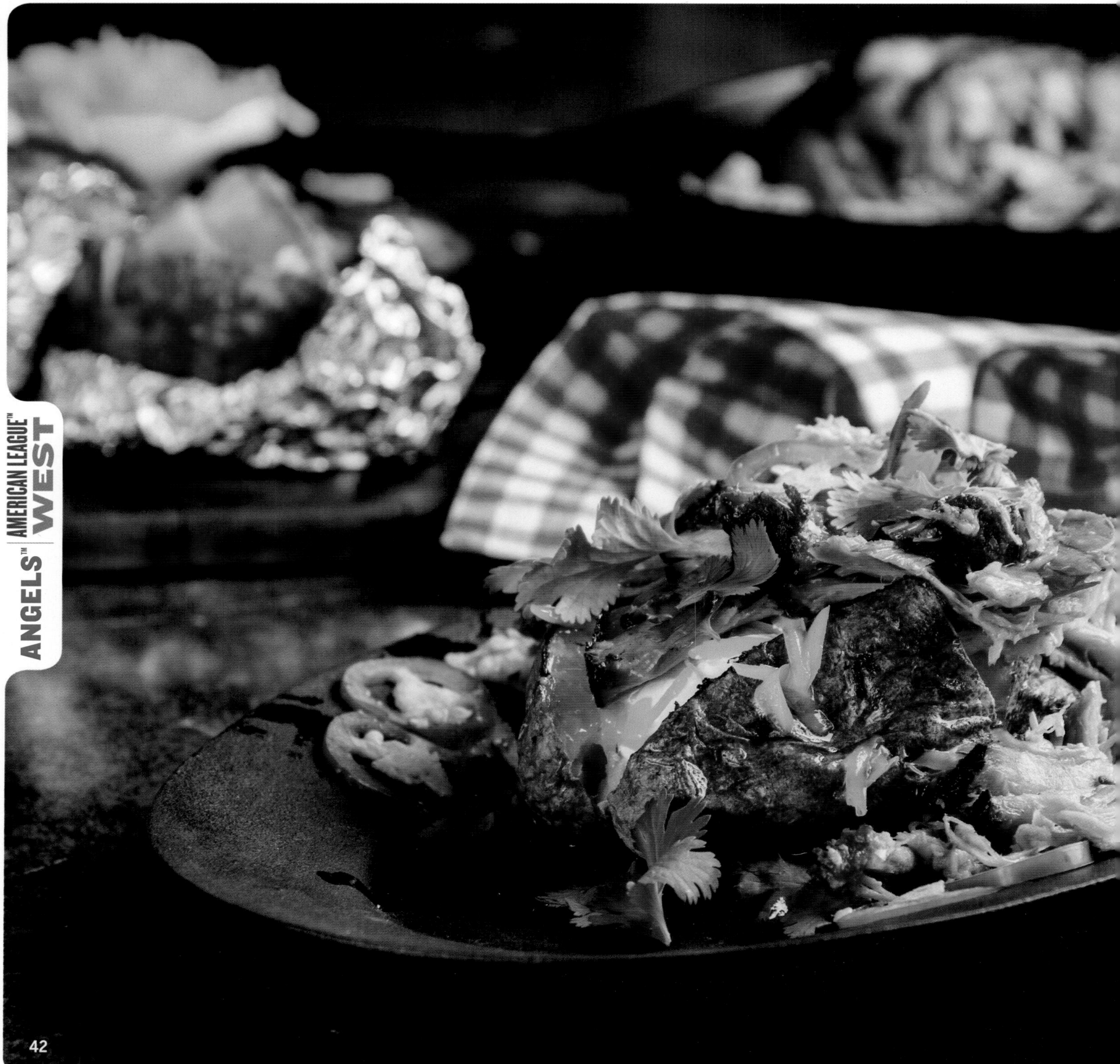

BARBECUE BAKED POTATO
with Smoked Pork Shoulder

IN Southern California, a loaded spud is quickly becoming a ballpark favorite. Our take on the ultimate baked potato features a whole grilled spud, split open, piled high with smoky pork shoulder, and loaded with toppings you'd find in your favorite taqueria.

1 In a small bowl, combine the brown sugar and all of the spices. Rub on all sides of the pork and set aside.

2 To prepare the grill for smoking, configure charcoals using the snake method, and add Kingsford™ Wood Chips along the line of coals.

3 Place a foil pan with hot water in the center of the snake. Light about eight briquets in a chimney. When ready, pile all of the lit coals at the head of the charcoal snake. The coals will burn down slowly as the meat cooks.

4 Place the pork shoulder fat side up on the rack, cover with the lid, and bring the temperature up to a constant 250 degrees Fahrenheit, using the vents to regulate heat.

5 Check the temperature of the grill every hour, adding more charcoal and wood chips as needed to maintain heat.

6 Smoke for 8–9 hours, or until the internal temperature of the pork reaches about 205 degrees Fahrenheit. Carefully remove from the grill and let rest for at least 15 minutes before shredding into large chunks.

7 To cook the potatoes, remove the wood chips and prepare the charcoal fire for indirect cooking, situating the coals on one side of the grill. Preheat to 450 degrees Fahrenheit.

8 Wash the potatoes and wrap each one in foil. Place over indirect heat, away from the coals, and close the lid. Cook until the potatoes soften, about 1 hour and 30 minutes.

9 Transfer the potatoes to a cutting board. Slit the top of each potato and fill with butter, sour cream, jalapeños, cheese and avocados.

10 Top each with about 3/4 cup of pulled pork and garnish with cilantro.

MAKES	PREP TIME	COOK TIME
4 servings	**15** minutes	**9–11** hours

2	tablespoons dark brown sugar
1	tablespoon kosher salt
1	teaspoon black pepper
1	teaspoon garlic powder
1	teaspoon onion powder
1	teaspoon smoked paprika
¼	teaspoon cayenne pepper
1	7-pound pork shoulder
4	large baking potatoes
4	tablespoons butter
¼	cup plus 2 tablespoons sour cream
1	jalapeño pepper, thinly sliced
1	cup shredded cheddar cheese
1	large avocado, diced
	Freshly chopped cilantro, for garnish
	Kingsford™ Wood Chips with Hickory

43

MAKES	PREP TIME	COOK TIME
4-6 servings	**15** minutes + marinating time	**1½** hours

3	tablespoons yellow mustard
¼	cup beer* (microbrewery IPA of choice)
1 ½	tablespoons Worcestershire sauce
2	pounds trimmed prime grade beef tri-tip, silver skin removed
2	teaspoons kosher salt
1	teaspoon freshly ground black pepper
1	tablespoon granulated garlic
	Neutral cooking oil for grilling, as needed
1	teaspoon flaky Maldon salt or fleur de sel, for finishing

ORIGINAL NOR-CAL BBQ TRI-TIP

Sports fans of Oakland, California are famous for their tailgating, and this recipe is a good example of how they'll elevate a cookout classic with a couple of upgraded ingredients. If you don't have a favorite IPA, ask a microbrew-loving friend. You won't be disappointed.

1 In a small bowl, whisk together the mustard, beer and Worcestershire sauce. Spread the mixture all over the tri-tip. Season the tri-tip all over with 2 teaspoons salt, 1 teaspoon pepper, and the granulated garlic.

2 Place the tri-tip in a plastic bag or large dish and let it rest and marinate for at least 30 minutes in the refrigerator. You may also let it marinate, refrigerated, for several hours and up to overnight.

3 When ready to cook, light a full chimney of Kingsford® Charcoal or a pile of about 100 briquets. Build a two-zone fire, placing preheated briquets on one half of the bottom grill grate and leaving the other side void.

4 Replace the grate, allow it to heat up to 400 degrees Fahrenheit—all vents should be fully open—then pour cooking oil on a folded paper towel and oil the grate using long-handled tongs.

5 For more intense smoke flavor, add about two cups of Kingsford™ Wood Chips with Hickory or Mesquite. Be sure to soak the chips for at least 30 minutes in water before spreading on the coals.

6 Place the tri-tip on the warm side of the grate (not directly over the coals), close the lid, and grill it for about 20–30 minutes, then turn it over and repeat.

7 When the tri-tip is close to your desired internal temperature, 140 degrees for medium, remove the lid and sear both sides directly over the coals, for about 3 to 4 minutes per side. For your safety, please reference the USDA safe cooking temperatures.

8 After the tri-tip comes off the grill, cover loosely with foil and let it rest for about 10 minutes.

9 Once rested, cut in half along the grain and then slice, very thinly, against the grain. Dip each slice into the collected juices created by slicing and serve, sprinkled with finishing salt.

*Recipes containing alcohol are intended only for those 21 years of age and older. Please drink responsibly.

45

SMOKED OYSTERS *with Spicy Miso Butter*

SEATTLE MARINERS | AMERICAN LEAGUE" WEST

MAKES	PREP TIME	COOK TIME
24 oysters	**30** minutes	**20** minutes

24	fresh, live oysters
6	tablespoons (3/4 stick) butter, at room temperature
2	tablespoons white miso
1to2	tablespoons Sriracha, more if you like it spicy
1	tablespoon fresh lime juice, plus wedges for serving
	Freshly ground pepper, to taste
1	bunch scallions, thinly sliced on a slight diagonal
	Togarashi seasoning, to taste

IF you've ever visited the tuna-tossing fishmongers at Seattle's Pike Place Market, you know the Pacific Northwest boasts some of the freshest seafood in the country. Give this smoky, miso-infused recipe a try the next time you score a fresh batch of live oysters.

1 Check to see if the oysters are alive by confirming that shells are tightly closed; discard any that are not tightly closed. Scrub oysters with a stiff brush under running water. Rinse well and refrigerate until ready to grill.

2 In a small bowl, beat together the softened butter, miso, Sriracha and lime juice with a spoon. Add a few grinds of black pepper and set aside in the fridge.

3 Build a charcoal fire for direct grilling using Kingsford® Charcoal and preheat to 450 degrees Fahrenheit.

4 Pry oyster shells apart with an oyster knife. Discard the top shell and loosen the oyster meat with the tip of the oyster knife.

5 Leave the oysters in the bottom shells and place oysters directly over coals with their deeply curved half shells facing upward; grill for approximately 3 minutes.

6 Top each oyster with approximately 1/2 teaspoon of spicy miso butter, adjusting for size of the oysters. Place oysters back on grill for an additional 3 minutes. For your safety, please reference the USDA safe cooking temperatures.

7 Serve in the half shell with the scallions scattered over the top and sprinkled with few good pinches of togarashi. Serve with lime wedges.

BASES LOADED SANDWICHES:
Bacon, Baloney and Brisket

TEXAS RANGERS

Yes, everything really is bigger in Texas, which is why fans there are lining up for a massive bacon, baloney and brisket sandwich that could only come from the Lone Star State. Our version features a drizzle of KC Masterpiece® Barbecue sauce to sweeten up that smoky mountain of savory meats.

1. Crush the beef bouillon cubes and mix with Worcestershire sauce. Cover the entire brisket with the wet rub. Mix the salt, pepper, brown sugar, smoked paprika, onion powder and garlic powder, and rub all over the brisket.

2. Using Kingsford® Charcoal, prepare the grill for indirect cooking, situating the coals on one side of the grill. Preheat to 225 degrees Fahrenheit.

3. Place the brisket on the grill, not directly over the coals, with fat side up. Cook for about 5 hours until the internal temperature of the brisket reaches 185 to 190 degrees Fahrenheit. Add wood chips during the initial cooking process to increase smoke flavor.

4. Double a large piece of aluminum foil and place brisket, fat side down, in the center. Boat the sides of the foil and pour 1 cup of water over the brisket. Wrap aluminum foil tightly around the entire brisket and place in cooker for 1–2 more hours. Internal temperature of the brisket should reach 185 to 190 degrees Fahrenheit when removed from the cooker.

5. Let the meat rest for 1–2 hours in the foil before unwrapping. Remove the brisket from the foil and slice across the grain of the meat.

6. While the meat is resting, preheat the oven to 400 degress Fahrenheit. Line a baking sheet with foil and top with a rack that fits inside the sheet.

7. Lay the bacon slices in a single layer on the rack. Bake for about 15–18 minutes, until browned but not too crisp. For your safety, please reference the USDA safe cooking temperatures.

8. While the bacon is cooking and when the brisket is done resting, raise the temperature of the grill. Place the baloney directly over the coals and grill until slightly charred, about 2–3 minutes per side.

9. To build the sandwiches, spread barbecue sauce onto buns. Add one slice of baloney, and top with about 3/4 cup chopped brisket. Add another slice of baloney, followed by 2–3 slices of bacon.

10. Drizzle with more sauce and close with the top half of the bun. Serve immediately.

2	teaspoons Worcestershire sauce	½	teaspoon garlic powder
4	beef bouillon cubes	1	pound bacon
1	6-pound brisket	12	slices baloney, about 1/4-inch thick each
½	tablespoon salt		
1	teaspoon black pepper	4	Kaiser rolls or large hamburger buns
1	teaspoon brown sugar		
½	tablespoon smoked paprika	½	cup KC Masterpiece® Original Barbecue Sauce
½	teaspoon onion powder		

MAKES
6
servings

PREP TIME
15
minutes

COOK TIME
6-8
hours

National

LEAGUE

> "In some places it's hot dogs. In others, it's hamburgers. But in my home country, in my memory, it's arepas. They will always mean baseball to me."

OMAR VIZQUEL

VENEZUELA

During his youth in Caracas, Venezuela, Omar Vizquel could smell the baseball stadium before he could see it as he made his way to practice. His bat slung across his shoulder, he would pick up the unmistakable aromas of smoke and meat.

Vizquel knew the source: a small food cart parked by the third-base dugout. Its operator was a friendly older man, whose specialty was arepas, a Venezuelan staple forever linked to baseball in Vizquel's mind.

"At any baseball stadium anywhere you always have the smell of foods that greet you," Vizquel says. "In some places it's hot dogs, or hamburgers or cheesesteak sandwiches. But in my home country, it's arepas. They will always mean baseball to me."

A three-time All-Star and 11-time Gold Glove winner during a 24-year big-league career, Vizquel brought more than just a terrific glove to work. He led the American League in sacrifice hits four times and developed into a prolific base-stealer.

Arepas are as versatile a dish as Vizquel was a ballplayer. In every version, the centerpiece is a round, flat patty of cornmeal or flour that can be steamed, boiled, fried, baked or grilled. It's the accompaniments that vary. Arepas can be stuffed or filled with almost whatever you desire.

At Estadio Universitario, Vizquel's boyhood ballpark, the old man in the food cart made arepas with chicken, cheese and beef, grilling the ingredients on a cast-iron skillet. Vizquel would take his cuts in batting practice, then hustle down the third-base line to grab a bite to eat, often joined by teammates, bat boys and clubhouse attendants. On game days, spectators would crowd the food cart, too.

For Vizquel, the arepas he ate at home represented the lone rival to those he had at the ballpark. He and his younger brother and their parents grew up in a two-bedroom apartment. His father was an electrician and his mother ran the house and ruled the kitchen. She made a mean roast chicken, and a tasty pabellon criollo, a traditional stew of rice, black beans and shredded beef. In the morning, she prepared arepas with leftover meat from the previous night.

There wasn't much money for dining out. But on special occasions, like birthdays and anniversaries, Vizquel's mom made feasts worthy of the finest local restaurants. They revolved around such dishes as seared ribeye with avocado sauce called guasacaca, and crispy-skin chicken spiked with aguita de sapo, a lively condiment made from garlic, cilantro and lime. These festive meals never failed to draw a crowd. Grandparents. Cousins. Friends from down the street. Everyone was welcome.

"A big meal was like a baseball game," Vizquel says. "It became a big neighborhood event."

This was the sweet life Vizquel left behind when he moved to the United States. His first stop on his path to the big leagues was Butte, Mont., where he played on a farm team with several other players from Latin America. Some teammates cooked meals inspired by their youths in Puerto Rico, Mexico and the Dominican Republic. It wasn't the same food he ate growing up, but it had a ring of familiarity to it.

"You'd have some guys in the kitchen and other guys doing laundry or washing the dishes," Vizquel says. "This was my new family. My baseball family."

Over the years, his baseball family grew. Vizquel formed special bonds with fellow baseball stars from Venezuela. When their schedules overlapped, they would throw dinners at one another's houses, typically at big houses with big barbecue setups. They would kick back and throw big steaks on the grill.

"Guys like Miguel Cabrera and Anibal Sanchez, they were always really generous like that," Vizquel says. "They really loved to grill."

Vizquel has since become an avid cook himself, preparing arepas and other specialties. He cooks them for his wife and children, as well as for his mom when she visits the family. Even if he can't quite match her prowess, he insists on doing the cooking.

"When she's in my home, I want her to relax," he says. "I don't want her to do any work. I want to cook for her. It's one way I can return all the love she gave to me."

Coal Fired CHICKEN AREPAS

Miami

On the streets of the Magic City, these South American stuffed cornmeal patties are king. We fill our arepas with savory grilled chicken, along with a creamy avocado salad that packs just the right amount of jalapeño bite.

1 Whisk together 3 tablespoons oil, 2 tablespoons lime juice, Worcestershire sauce, half the garlic, brown sugar, cumin, 1 teaspoon salt and 1 teaspoon pepper in a small bowl.

2 Place chicken and marinade in large resealable plastic bag. Seal, removing as much air as possible, and refrigerate for at least 4 hours.

3 Whisk together cornmeal and 1 teaspoon of salt in medium bowl. Add 2½ cups lukewarm water. Stir until combined; let sit 5 minutes.

4 Use wet hands to knead dough until smooth. Divide dough into 8 portions; roll portions into balls.

5 Meanwhile, heat about 1 tablespoon oil in large cast iron or non-stick skillet over the grill.

6 Add balls in batches, leaving at least 3 inches between each one. Using the palm of your hand, flatten balls to 1/2-inch thick. Cook, flipping once, until golden brown on both sides and heated through, about 5 to 6 minutes on each

side. Repeat with remaining dough, adding more oil as needed. Cut arepas in half horizontally without detaching ends.

7 Build a charcoal fire for direct grilling using Kingsford® Charcoal and preheat to 400 degrees Fahrenheit.

8 In a medium bowl, mix diced avocado with mayonnaise and remaining lime juice and garlic. Add the onion, jalapeño (if using) and cilantro. Salt and pepper to taste. Cover and store in the fridge until ready to eat.

9 Remove chicken from the marinade, shaking off excess. Discard marinade. Place thighs on the grill over direct heat for 6 to 8 minutes per side until golden brown and firm to the touch. Remove the chicken from the grill and cut into thin strips.

10 Fill the arepas with the grilled chicken and avocado salad. Serve immediately.

3	tablespoons olive oil, plus more for cooking arepas
3	tablespoons fresh lime juice, divided
2	tablespoons Worcestershire sauce
4	cloves garlic, finely minced, divided
1	teaspoon brown sugar
1	teaspoon ground cumin
2	teaspoons kosher salt, divided
1	teaspoon freshly ground black pepper
1 ¼	pounds boneless, skinless chicken thighs
2	cups precooked white cornmeal (such as Harina P.A.N.® or ArepArina)
2	ripe Haas avocados, roughly diced
3	tablespoons mayonnaise
¼	cup finely diced white onion
1	medium jalapeño, stemmed seeded and finely chopped (optional)
½	cup packed roughly chopped fresh cilantro leaves

MIAMI MARLINS™ | **NATIONAL LEAGUE™ EAST**

MAKES	PREP TIME	COOK TIME
4-6 servings	**15** minutes	**20** minutes

4	ripe peaches, peeled, pitted and roughly chopped
½	cup pure maple syrup
2	tablespoons lemon juice
¼	cup bourbon*
1	tablespoon apple cider vinegar
1	clove garlic, minced
2	teaspoons whole grain mustard
	Kosher salt, to taste
	Ground black pepper, to taste
4	double cut (tomahawk) pork chops, frenched (about 1½–2 inches thick)
1 ½	teaspoons granulated garlic
1 ½	teaspoons smoked paprika
2	scallions, sliced, for garnish

GRILLED TOMAHAWK PORK CHOPS *with Peach Bourbon Glaze*

Nobody knows the tomahawk like Atlanta's baseball fanatics, and these fired up pork chops feature a sweet secret—a peach bourbon glaze you'll want to brush onto everything you grill. Be sure to serve up a little glaze on the side for dipping and drizzling.

1 To make the glaze, place the peaches, maple syrup, lemon juice, bourbon, apple cider vinegar, garlic and mustard in a small saucepan over medium heat.

2 Bring to a simmer and cook, stirring occasionally and mashing the peaches, until the fruit has softened and the alcohol has mostly cooked off about 5–7 minutes.

3 Season to taste with salt and pepper. For a completely smooth glaze, transfer to a blender and puree. Divide glaze in two; half for basting and half for garnishing.

4 Using Kingsford® Charcoal, build a charcoal fire for direct grilling, and preheat to 400 degrees Fahrenheit. Oil the grates to prevent sticking.

5 Season the chops well on both sides with the salt, pepper, granulated garlic and smoked paprika.

6 Grill chops directly over coals for 7–8 minutes on each side, or until the internal temperature reaches about 155 degrees Fahrenheit.

7 During the last 4 minutes of cooking, baste both sides of the chops a few times with the glaze. Remove and let rest for at least 5 minutes. Discard any remaining basting glaze.

8 Garnish with scallions and serve hot, with remaining glaze on the side.

*Recipes containing alcohol are intended only for those 21 years of age and older. Please drink responsibly.

FILET STEAK SANDWICH

MAKES	PREP TIME	COOK TIME
4 sandwiches	**20** minutes	**15** minutes

1	cup beef stock
1	teaspoon granulated garlic
1 ½	teaspoons balsamic glaze
4	5–6-ounce filet mignon steaks, about 1½ inches thick
	Kosher salt, to taste
	Ground black pepper, to taste
2	sweet onions, sliced into 1/2-inch-thick rounds
1–2	long and wide baguettes (or Italian bread), cut into 4 6-inch sections
2	tablespoons olive oil, plus more for brushing the bread
4	slices provolone cheese

Nothing gets New Yorkers excited like a great sandwich, and this ballpark beauty does the trick. Our elevated twist on the humble hot beef features a luxurious slab of filet mignon, plenty of sweet onions, and a gooey layer of provolone cheese on a crispy baguette.

1 Build a two-zone fire using Kingsford® Charcoal for indirect grilling by situating heated coals on only one side of the grill, leaving the other side empty. Preheat to 450 degrees Fahrenheit. Lightly grease the grates to prevent sticking.

2 To make the au jus sauce, warm the beef stock, garlic and balsamic glaze in a small pot on the stove. Set aside.

3 Season the steaks generously on both sides with salt and pepper. Place directly over the coals and cook for about 8 minutes total, flipping once halfway through, until charred on both sides.

4 Move the steaks to the unheated side of the grill to finish with indirect cooking. Grill until the steaks reach desired doneness, about 125 degrees Fahrenheit for medium rare. For your safety, please reference the USDA safe cooking temperatures. Remove from grill and let rest for 10 minutes.

5 Cut into thin slices, and toss with the au jus.

6 While the steak is cooking, brush the onion slices with oil, season with salt and pepper and grill them, turning a few times until they're softened and charred.

7 Prepare the rolls by brushing cut sides with oil and grill (cut sides down) until the bread is lightly toasted.

8 To build the sandwiches, divide the meat between the toasted rolls, spooning a little extra jus over the meat and bread. Top with grilled onions and a slice of provolone cheese.

9 Move the sandwiches back to the grill and cover just until the cheese is melted. Serve hot.

BURNT ENDS CHEESESTEAK

Our tailgate-tested take on Philly's classic is certainly inspired by the iconic sandwiches they serve up at the city's revered cheesesteak joints, but we've swapped out thin slices of rib-eye with succulent, chunky burnt ends.

1   To make the dry rub, mix the first eight ingredients until well combined in a small bowl. Set aside.

2   Prepare charcoal in a snake configuration, and add Kingsford™ Wood Chips along the line of coals. Place a foil pan with hot water in the center of the snake.

3   Light about eight briquets in a chimney. When ready, pile all of the lit coals at the head of the charcoal snake. The coals will burn down slowly as the meat cooks.

4   Trim all fat from the brisket point and season generously with dry rub. Place seasoned point in the smoker, cover and cook for five hours. Remove the point from the smoker and wrap it in a layer of foil, then return to the smoker.

5   Allow the point to cook until it reaches an internal temperature of 210 degrees Fahrenheit. Pressing with your finger, the point should have some resistance, but should be soft to the touch.

6   Let the wrapped point cool on the counter for 10–15 minutes before cutting. Slice into cubes 1-inch by 1-inch. Reserve the natural juices retained in the wrap, and toss burnt end cubes in the au jus.

7 While the brisket is finishing cooking, warm the oil in a large skillet over low heat. Add onions and cook 8 to 10 minutes, until caramelized and softened. Stir frequently and avoid browning.

8 Transfer onions to a bowl; add peppers to same skillet, still over low heat. Cook peppers 10 to 15 minutes until soft and tender, flipping often. Transfer to bowl with onions. Season onion-pepper mixture to taste. Cover bowl to keep warm.

9 Prepare the rolls by brushing cut sides with oil and grill (cut sides down) until the bread is lightly toasted. Distribute burnt ends between the rolls, and top with the onions and pepper mixture.

10 Add the cheese to the sandwich, and return to the grill until the cheese is just melted. Serve hot.

MAKES	PREP TIME	COOK TIME
6 sandwiches	**20** minutes	**6–7** hours

¼	cup light brown sugar
2	tablespoons smoked paprika
1	tablespoon kosher salt
2	teaspoons ground black pepper
1 ½	teaspoons chili powder
1 ½	teaspoons garlic powder
1 ½	teaspoons onion powder
¼	teaspoon cayenne pepper
1	4-pound brisket point
2	tablespoons olive oil
1	large yellow onion, sliced thin
2	red peppers, sliced
1	green pepper, sliced
	Kosher salt, to taste
	Ground black pepper, to taste
6	hero or hard rolls, each about 6 inches long, split
6	slices Swiss, American or provolone cheese

GRILLED CHICKEN SOUVLAKI SKEWERS

with Chopped Greek Salad

reek food has been a staple of DC culture for decades, so it's no surprise that easy-to-eat souvlaki skewers are a favorite in the streets and at the ballpark. We like to serve ours hot off the grill, on top of a cool cucumber and tomato salad.

1 For the skewers, combine the lemon juice and zest, olive oil, oregano, garlic, and plenty of salt and pepper. Add the cubed chicken and toss to coat evenly. Marinate in the refrigerator for at least 30 minutes, or up to one hour.

2 Divide chicken pieces into 8 portions and thread onto the skewers.

3 While the chicken is marinating, make the salad. In a medium bowl, combine the tomatoes, cucumbers, red onions, lemon juice, olive oil and oregano. Season to taste with salt and pepper. Set aside.

4 Build a charcoal fire for direct grilling using Kingsford® Charcoal and preheat to 400 degrees Fahrenheit. Lightly oil the grates to prevent sticking.

5 Place the chicken skewers on the grill and cook for 10–12 minutes, turning often, until the chicken is cooked through. For your safety, please reference the USDA safe cooking temperatures.

6 Serve the skewers warm on top of the salad.

MAKES	PREP TIME	COOK TIME
8	**30**	**12**
skewers	minutes plus marinating time	minutes

For the Chicken

¼	cup lemon juice
2	tablespoons lemon zest
¼	cup plus 2 tablespoons extra-virgin olive oil
2	teaspoons dried oregano
3	garlic cloves, minced
	Kosher salt and ground black pepper, to taste
2	pounds boneless, skinless chicken breast, cut into 1-inch cubes
8	wooden skewers, soaked in water for at least 20 minutes

For the Salad

2	cups tomato, diced
2	cups cucumber, diced
½	cup red onion, minced
3	tablespoons fresh lemon juice
3	tablespoons olive oil
1	teaspoon dried oregano
	Kosher salt and ground black pepper, to taste

> "To this day, anytime someone mentions barbecue, the first things I think of are baseball and my dad."

HAROLD REYNOLDS

1869 - 1969

UNITED STATES 6c

PROFESSIONAL BASEBALL

AMERICAN

BAR-B-QUE

During a 12-year big-league career that included three Gold Gloves, two-time All-Star Harold Reynolds ate his best home-cooked meals on the road.

On team trips to Oakland, where his father, John, resided, Reynolds knew he could count on two things: tough games vs. the Athletics, and heaping portions of fork-tender pork ribs.

"My dad had one of those big, gray egg-shaped smokers, and he'd get that thing cranked up a few days before we got to town,"

Reynolds says. "By the time we showed up, he'd have big trays of ribs laid out for us in the clubhouse. Guys would be sitting around eating them all day."

Reynolds says his father never shared his "secret recipe." But it involved dry-rub marinade, set in the refrigerator overnight, followed by low, slow-cooking that left the meat all but falling off the bone, with a hint of smoky flavor and a trace of teriyaki-like sweetness. Reynolds and his teammates inhaled so many of them you would have thought the ribs were sunflower seeds.

The only other place where Reynolds tasted barbecue just like it was in Detroit, where his Uncle Bob, a master of the same pork rib recipe, lived. He also provided clubhouse feasts.

"It got to the point where guys would be looking at the schedule and saying, 'Hey, we're going to Oakland. Your dad's got the ribs, right?,'" Reynolds says. "And, 'Hey, next up, Detroit. Is your uncle doing the ribs?'"

Ballplayers seldom talk about their superstitions, but they have an abundance of them. The Reynolds ribs became shrouded in superstition for one of the greatest ballplayers of his generation.

"The first time Ken Griffey, Jr. had the ribs, he homered the next day," Reynolds says of his former Seattle Mariners teammate. "So from then on it was, 'Where's that barbecue? We need to get some more of that barbecue.'"

Reynolds was not above clinging to superstition either. As a minor-league player in Salt Lake City, Reynolds dined at a local barbecue joint over a full plate then went to the ballpark and had a big night at the plate. The following night, he returned to the same restaurant with a few of his teammates. They also had big nights at the plate. Word spread quickly. It wasn't long before the entire starting lineup had a favorite place to eat.

"Baseball is like that," Reynolds says. "There are all sorts of customs and rituals around it, and food is often a big part of them."

The youngest of eight children raised in Eugene, Ore., Reynolds recalls a childhood filled with family gatherings with baseball on

TV and good stuff on the grill. Warm-weather holidays, including Memorial Day and Fourth of July, gave rise to large outdoor celebrations.

"Hot dogs, hamburgers, chicken, you name it," Reynolds says. "But it was lots of people, and lots and lots of food. I remember one time someone cooked the whole pig."

Reynolds developed a silver palate for various barbecue styles to go with his Gold Gloves. When forced to state a preference, Reynolds says he leans toward the slightly sweet and sticky barbecue of Kansas City. But he sees plenty to like in the dry-rubbed meats of Texas, and in the vinegary tang of Carolina 'cue. Name a city and there's a good chance he can point you to a killer rib place, his favorite of all being in Minnesota.

"The first time I went to this place, Kirby Puckett and Prince were both there eating," Reynolds says. "I kept going back, hoping I'd see them again. I never did, but it doesn't matter. The food is THAT good."

Having taken his baseball knowledge from the field to the broadcast booth, Reynolds hasn't lost his taste for barbecue, or the festivities that come with it: backyard cookouts and clubhouse bashes. His uncle and his father both died some years ago, but his memories of them are alive and well.

"To this day," Reynolds says, "anytime someone mentions barbecue, the first things I think of are baseball and my dad."

ST. LOUIS BBQ RIBS

MAKES	PREP TIME	COOK TIME
4-6 servings	**30** minutes	**4-** to 4 1/2 hours

The people of St. Louis know their BBQ sauce, and when they talk BBQ, they're actually talkin' grilled pork ribs, smothered in a sweet, smoky layer of deliciousness that you'll want to pour over everything. Take our advice, and make plenty of extra sauce and dry rub to store away for later..

1 Prepare the rub: In a medium bowl, whisk all rub ingredients together. Use your fingertips to break up any large clumps of brown sugar.

2 Set aside 2 tablespoons rub to use in sauce and apply the rest of the rub to front and back of ribs.

3 Build a charcoal fire using Kingsford® Charcoal for indirect grilling by situating the coals on only one side of the grill, leaving the other side void. Preheat to 250 degrees Fahrenheit.

4 Once the grill is preheated, place the ribs on the grill meat-side up and cook with indirect heat for 3½–4 hours, or until the ribs are tender. For your

safety, please reference the USDA safe cooking temperatures.

5 While ribs are cooking, make the sauce by combining all the sauce ingredients into a medium saucepan along with the 2 tablespoons reserved spice rub.

6 Stir in 1/2 cup water and bring to a boil over high heat, reduce heat and simmer for 8 to 10 minutes, stirring often, until reduced to a glaze consistency. Sauce should reduce by about one-third. Remove from heat and allow the sauce to cool.

7 During the last 30 minutes of cooking, brush the sauce on to both sides of the ribs in two coats. Discard any leftover sauce after use; do not reuse or re-boil sauce.

8 Remove the ribs from the grill and place them on a cutting board to rest for about 10 minutes. Carve the ribs and serve.

2	slabs St. Louis-style cut ribs, membrane removed from underside of ribs, any loose fat or meat trimmed

For the Spice Rub

¼	cup brown sugar
2	tablespoons onion powder
2	tablespoons smoked paprika
1	tablespoons dry mustard
½	tablespoon garlic powder
½	tablespoon dried oregano
1	teaspoon ground coriander
½	teaspoon cayenne pepper
2	tablespoons kosher salt
1	tablespoon freshly ground black pepper

For the Sauce

2 ½	cups ketchup
⅓	cup apple cider vinegar
¼	cup brown sugar
¼	cup molasses
2	tablespoons Dijon mustard
1	tablespoon Worcestershire sauce
1	teaspoon liquid smoke (optional)

CHICAGO-STYLE CHAR DOG

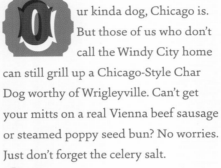

Our kinda dog, Chicago is. But those of us who don't call the Windy City home can still grill up a Chicago-Style Char Dog worthy of Wrigleyville. Can't get your mitts on a real Vienna beef sausage or steamed poppy seed bun? No worries. Just don't forget the celery salt.

1. Build a charcoal fire for direct grilling using Kingsford® Charcoal and preheat to 400 degrees Fahrenheit. Lightly oil the grates to prevent sticking.

2. Butterfly hot dogs by slicing them lengthwise without cutting all the way through. Open gently so they lay flat on the grill.

3. Cook for about 2–3 minutes on each side, until charred in spots and hot throughout. For your safety, please reference the USDA safe cooking temperatures.

4. While the grill is heating and the hot dogs are cooking, grill the buns quickly over direct heat until lightly toasted, about 1 minute.

5. Place one hot dog in each bun, and top with a quarter of the mustard, relish, onions, tomatoes and one pickle spear. Add sport peppers, to taste, and sprinkle with celery salt.

6. Repeat with remaining hot dogs and serve immediately.

CHICAGO CUBS™ | NATIONAL LEAGUE™ CENTRAL

MAKES	PREP TIME	COOK TIME
4 servings	**10** minutes	**3–5** minutes

4	all-beef hot dogs
4	hot dog buns
2	tablespoons yellow mustard
¼	cup bright green sweet pickle relish
½	small white onion, diced
2	small Roma tomatoes, cut into thin wedges
4	dill pickle spears
	Pickled sport peppers, to taste
	Celery salt, to taste

½	pound ground lean pork
½	pound ground beef
¼	cup onion, finely diced
¾	cup quick cooking oats
1	egg, lightly beaten
2	teaspoons Worcestershire sauce
½	teaspoon garlic powder
½	teaspoon dried sage
½	teaspoon dried thyme
¼	teaspoon ground allspice
¼	teaspoon cayenne pepper
1	teaspoon kosher salt
½	teaspoon freshly ground black pepper
2	tablespoons melted butter, for bread
8	slices rye or pumpernickel marble bread
4	slices Swiss or Gruyere cheese
¼	cup Dijon mustard
1	cup sauerkraut, drained

MAKES **4** sandwiches | **PREP TIME** **15** minutes | **COOK TIME** **15** minutes

GRILLED GERMAN GOETTA BURGERS

For the good people of Cincinnati, goetta has always been the breakfast meat of choice. This burger is inspired by the city's rich German heritage and its favorite sausage, and features a 50/50 blend of ground pork and beef, along with plenty of savory spices.

1 In a large bowl, combine pork, beef, onion, oats, egg, Worcestershire sauce, and dried herbs and spices. Season with 1 teaspoon salt, 1/2 teaspoon pepper and use your hands to gently combine and incorporate all ingredients.

2 Form the mixture into 4 burger patties.

3 Meanwhile, prepare a grill using Kingsford® Charcoal, build a fire for direct grilling and preheat to 400 degrees Fahrenheit.

4 Place the burgers on the grill and cook them until browned and cooked through, flipping once halfway through, 8 to 10 minutes total. For your safety, please reference the USDA safe cooking temperatures. Remove patties from grill, allow to rest for 3 minutes.

5 Brush the bread slices with butter and toast them on the grill, a minute or two each side. Add a slice of cheese for the last minute and let it melt slightly.

6 Spread Dijon onto half the toasted bread.

7 Place the burgers on the mustard, top with sauerkraut and the other slice of toasted bread. Serve immediately.

BEER & CHEESE SAUCED BRATS

IF you love Milwaukee, chances are good that you love beer, cheese and sausage. This game-ready recipe is a celebration of all three. Frankly, we'd eat anything smothered in our roux-based cheese sauce, especially brats cooked in beer and grilled over a flame.

1. Build a two-zone fire using Kingsford® Charcoal for indirect grilling by situating heated coals on only one side of the grill. Preheat to 350 degrees Fahrenheit.

2. In a medium saucepan, melt the butter over the void side of the grill. Whisk in the flour and cook for 1 minute. Add half and half, and cook until thickened a bit, whisking constantly, 1 to 2 minutes.

3. Once hot and thickened, add the mustard and slowly whisk in 4 ounces (1/2 cup) beer. Continue to cook until very hot.

4. Lower the heat and toss the cheese in a bowl with the cornstarch. Slowly add the cornstarch/cheese to the sauce, whisking well to incorporate after each addition, until melted.

5. Remove sauce from heat, season with salt, pepper and a pinch of cayenne or hot sauce to taste, and set aside.

6. Place remaining beer and brats in an oven-proof pan and place onto the grill. Boil brats in the beer for 10 to 15 minutes, or until the brats turn white. Use a pair of long-handled tongs to move and rotate your brats, being careful not to pierce or break the skin.

7 Meanwhile brush the onion slices with oil and grill them, turning a few times until they're softened and charred.

8 Move the pan over to the cool side and remove the sausages, placing them directly over the coals. Rotate brats to avoid burning. You want even grill marks on all sides, 10 to 12 minutes. For your safety, please reference the USDA safe cooking temperatures.

9 Prepare rolls by brushing cut sides with oil and grill (cut sides down) until the bread is lightly toasted.

10 Cut the rested sausages diagonally into 3/4-inch slices, and divide among the toasted rolls. Top with the grilled onions and top with beer-cheese sauce. Serve, with additional beer-cheese sauce on the side.

MAKES	PREP TIME	COOK TIME
6 sandwiches	**25** minutes	**45** minutes

1	tablespoon butter
2	tablespoons flour
¾	cup half and half, warmed
1	tablespoon spicy brown mustard
12	ounces (1½ cups) room temperature beer*, divided
8	ounces grated sharp cheddar cheese
2	teaspoons cornstarch
½	teaspoon kosher salt
¼	teaspoon freshly ground black pepper
	Cayenne pepper or hot sauce, to taste
6	bratwurst sausages
1	cup beer
2	onions, sliced ½-inch thick
	Vegetable oil, as needed
6	hero or hard rolls, each about 6 inches long, split

*Recipes containing alcohol are intended only for those 21 years of age and older. Please drink responsibly.

79

CHEESESTEAK BURGERS with Fries & Coleslaw

The good people of Pittsburgh don't mess around. They work hard. They play hard. They stack their sandwiches high, and fill them with fries. Frankly, we don't know why we all don't turn our favorite side dishes into toppings.

1 To make the coleslaw, place the cabbage in a bowl. Toss with the apple cider vinegar and oil, and season to taste with salt and pepper. Set aside, stirring occasionally to make sure the slaw stays evenly coated.

2 Make the french fries according to package directions. If they are not seasoned well enough, add a little bit of salt when they come out of the oven.

3 Using Kingsford® Charcoal, build a charcoal fire for direct grilling and preheat to 400 degrees Fahrenheit. Lightly oil the grates to prevent sticking.

4 Shape the beef into 4 equal patties. Season generously with salt and pepper and indent the center of each one slightly so they don't shrink on the grill.

5 Add the burgers and cook, flipping once, about 6 minutes per side for medium doneness. In the last two minutes of cooking, add a slice of cheese to each burger and close the grill, cooking just until melted.

For your safety, please reference the USDA safe cooking temperatures.

6 To build the burgers, toast the bread and spread about 1 tablespoon of mayonnaise on four slices of bread. Top each with a burger patty, tomato slices, a quarter of the coleslaw and a handful of fries.

7 Cover with the remaining bread slices and serve immediately.

MAKES	PREP TIME	COOK TIME
4 servings	**20** minutes	**20–25 minutes**

1 ½	cups green cabbage, shredded
1 ½	tablespoons apple cider vinegar
1 ½	tablespoons light olive oil
	Kosher salt and ground black pepper, to taste
1 ½	pound bag frozen straight-cut french fries
1 ¼	pounds ground beef
4	slices cheddar cheese
8	slices Italian bread
¼	cup mayonnaise
1	large tomato, sliced

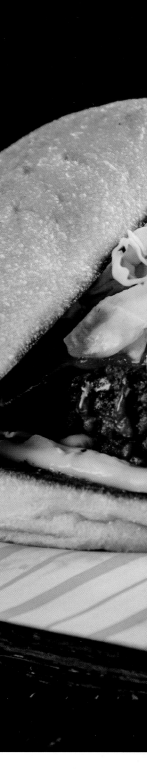

SOUTH KOREA

"To me, (grilling) it's a way of pausing, and getting away from all the distractions, ...It's a time to look around and really appreciate all that you have."

More than 20 years later, Byung-Hyun Kim remembers the ground beef on a bun.

It was 1996. Kim was a budding star in Korean youth baseball. The flight on his first trip to the United States had just touched down in Boston, where he would compete in an international junior tournament.

His schedule didn't allow for a sit-down meal, so he grabbed a burger on the go.

"To an American, it probably wouldn't have seemed like anything special," Kim says. "But I still remember how juicy and delicious it was. It was so much better than any meat I'd ever had back home."

Grilling plays a key role in Korean cooking, but Kim says meat was a rarity for him back then. His family was of modest means, so his mother built her meals around budget-minded staples: rice, vegetables and eggs. On birthdays and national holidays, Korean grilled beef and pork dishes such as bulgogi and galbi made their way onto the family table.

"I was always happy to eat whatever my mom served me," Kim

says. "But that's how it is when you're a kid. You only know what you know, and you don't really think about what you might be missing."

Pitching in the big leagues brought a world of new flavors to his plate. In Arizona, Kim's first stop in the Majors, Korean restaurants were still relatively rare. So Kim, eager to assimilate, eagerly embraced steakhouses, taco stands and burger joints. The more meat he ate, the more he craved it. The camaraderie that came with it was a welcome bonus. One day, a teammate brought a portable grill and hamburger meat to a practice. And just like that, Kim encountered his first spontaneous cookout outside the stadium.

"That experience was a real eye-opener for me," Kim says. "Up until that point, I'd only ever had hamburgers prepared for me in restaurants. This made me realize how much better a hamburger tastes when you make it yourself."

Though Kim wasn't a wizard in the kitchen, he knew enough to whip up simple dishes, such as grilled pork belly and marinated short ribs, which he served Korean-style, with kimchi and rice. He didn't have the space to throw big bashes, but sometimes brought his cooking into the clubhouse.

"Thing is, Korean food has a lot of garlic and spices," Kim says, "and that was too much for some of the guys."

Kim says he had little problem adapting to new foods, especially those prepared on a grill. He loved the aroma of fat and smoke that lingered in the air at big league stadiums, and the festive mood he sensed at tailgate parties. It was a side of baseball he had not known in Korea, where pregame barbecues were nowhere near as common. With little room around the stadiums, most people simply packed food and brought it to their seats.

"What struck me most in the United States was seeing how fans would slow things down," Kim says. "They'd be lounging on chairs or throwing the baseball around and listening to music, and just enjoying the moment. It was something new to me, and I really liked it."

Kim grew so accustomed to these easy-going customs that returning to Korea gave him reverse culture shock. He was accustomed to a faster pace, where everyone seemed to be in a rush. Kim says he made a point of trying to slow things down by grilling meals at home and by gathering with friends at Korean barbecue restaurants, where you grill your own meat on a tabletop hibachi, something of an indoor version of a tailgate party.

Upon moving to the States, Kim says he viewed grilling as a staple of success: He had come far enough in baseball that he could now afford some of the finer things in life.

Now, he sees it as something more important.

"To me, it's a way of pausing, and getting away from all the distractions," Kim says. "It's a time to look around and really appreciate all that you have."

SPICY KOREAN-STYLE CHICKEN WINGS

MAKES	PREP TIME	COOK TIME
4 servings	**30** minutes	**10** minutes

3	pounds chicken wings, separated into wings and drumettes
2	tablespoons extra-virgin olive oil
	Kosher salt, to taste
	Ground black pepper, to taste
3	cloves garlic, minced
1-	inch piece ginger, freshly grated
2	tablespoons sesame oil
¼	cup Gochujang (Korean chili paste)
¼	cup mirin
¼	cup soy sauce
2	tablespoons honey
2	scallions, thinly sliced, green parts only

 LA's Koreatown, the post-game meal of choice is a shared platter of garlicky, soy-infused wings inspired by the city's love for Asian flavors and spices. Find yourself a plastic tub of Gochujang chili paste, and be prepared to have your mind (and taste buds) blown.

1 Build a charcoal fire using Kingsford® Charcoal for indirect grilling by situating the coals on only one side of the grill, leaving the other side empty. Preheat to 350 degrees Fahrenheit.

2 Toss the wings in the oil and season with salt and pepper. Place them on the cool side of the grill and cook, covered, turning occasionally until the wings are cooked through, about 15–20 minutes. For your safety, please reference the USDA safe cooking temperatures.

3 Meanwhile, mix the garlic, ginger, sesame oil, Gochujang, mirin, soy sauce and honey in a bowl until well combined.

4 Toss the wings in the sauce to evenly coat. Remove wings from sauce and place back on the hot part of the grill.

5 Cook, turning often, for about 5 more minutes until glazed and browned.

6 Remove and garnish with sliced scallions. Serve immediately, with extra sauce if desired.

SMOKY RATTLE-SNAKE CHILI

IF you've ever tried rattlesnake meat, you know those cold-blooded critters are surprisingly tender. You can find smoked versions at some stores, or order deliveries online. If not, just substitute skinless chicken thighs. The chili powder and jalapeño still deliver plenty of bite.

1 Using Kingsford® Charcoal, build a fire for direct grilling and preheat to 400 degrees Fahrenheit.

2 Coat the snake meat and pork chops with 2 tablespoons of the oil, and season with 1 tablespoon of the chili powder, 1 teaspoon of the salt and the pepper.

3 Place the meat on the grill and cook for 8–10 minutes, turning once halfway through. It's ok if it's not fully cooked, it will finish in the chili.

4 While the meat cooks, brush the onions and peppers with 2 tablespoons of the oil and season with salt and pepper, to taste. Grill for about 8–10 minutes, turning once, until softened and charred in spots.

5 Transfer the meat, onions and peppers to the cutting board. Cut everything into diced pieces and mince the jalapeño.

6 Heat a large pot over medium-high heat. Add remaining oil, and when hot, add the meat, vegetables, canned tomatoes, remaining chili powder, salt, cumin, oregano, garlic and beef broth.

7 Bring to a boil with the grill's lid closed; then reduce heat and cook, stirring occasionally, for about 45 minutes to an hour, until everything is softened and comes together. For your safety, please reference the USDA safe cooking temperatures.

8 Add the beans in the last 15 minutes of cooking. Season to taste and serve hot, with cheese, sour cream, diced avocado and cilantro, for garnish.

ARIZONA DIAMONDBACKS™ | NATIONAL LEAGUE™ WEST

1	pound rattlesnake meat, skinned, boned and de-rattled (can sub boneless, skinless chicken thighs)
1	pound boneless pork loin chops
5	tablespoons olive oil, divided
2	tablespoons chili powder, divided
2	teaspoons kosher salt, divided, plus more to taste
1	teaspoon ground black pepper, plus more to taste
2	onions, cut into ½-inch slices
1	jalapeño pepper, stem removed
1	red pepper, stemmed, seeded and cut into 4 large pieces
1	green pepper, stemmed, seeded and cut into 4 large pieces
1	28-ounce can diced tomatoes
2	teaspoons cumin
2	teaspoons dried oregano
3	cloves minced garlic
1	cup beef broth
1	14-ounce can pinto or kidney beans, drained and rinsed
	Shredded cheese, sour cream, avocado and cilantro, for garnish

MAKES 6-8 servings | **PREP TIME** 25 minutes | **COOK TIME** 1 hour and 15 minutes

GRILLED
MOUNTAIN

90

ROCKY OYSTER PO'BOY

 et ready to have a fun conversation with your local butcher. Rocky Mountain oysters are actually animal testicles, typically of a calf or bull, although lamb, duck and buffalo can also be used. We recommend the smaller calf balls for this Rocky Mountain version of the "oyster" po'boy, and you won't find those shrink-wrapped next to the chicken thighs.

1 Using a sharp knife, gently peel the membrane off the Rocky Mountain oysters, and split in half lengthwise. Cover with the beer and let sit for one hour.

2 While the oysters are soaking, mash the avocados. Stir in the diced tomatoes, 1 tablespoon of the lime juice and plenty of salt to taste. Set aside.

3 In a separate bowl, make the slaw. Combine the cabbage, onion, jalapeño, 2 tablespoons of lime juice and 2 tablespoons olive oil. Season to taste with salt and pepper and set aside.

4 Using Kingsford® Charcoal, build a charcoal fire for direct grilling, and preheat to 350 degrees Fahrenheit. Oil the grates to prevent sticking.

5 Remove the oysters fro the beer, dry, and place in a bowl. Toss in the remaining olive oil. Season to taste with salt and pepper.

6 Place on the grill and cook until both sides are slightly charred and the insides are cooked through, about 8–10 minutes per side. For your safety, please reference the USDA safe cooking temperatures. Remove and sprinkle with remaining lime juice.

7 To build the sandwiches, lightly toast the sandwich rolls and spread an equal amount of mayonnaise on the inside of each. Divide the Rocky Mountain oysters between the rolls, and top with the slaw and guacamole.

8 Sprinkle with Cotija cheese, and garnish with cilantro, if desired. Serve immediately.

MAKES	PREP TIME	COOK TIME
4 Po'Boys	**30** minutes plus one hour soaking time	**20** minutes

2	pounds Rocky Mountain Oysters (calf testicles)
2	cups beer* (dark)
	kosher salt, to taste
	Ground black pepper, to taste
2	large avocados, peeled & pitted
2	large tomatoes, diced
¼	cup lime juice, divided
3	cups shredded green cabbage
½	small onion, julienned
½	jalapeño, minced
5	tablespoons extra-virgin olive oil, divided
4	long sandwich rolls, lightly toasted
⅓	cup mayonnaise
½	cup Cotija cheese
	Fresh cilantro, for garnish (optional)

*Recipes containing alcohol are intended only for those 21 years of age and older. Please drink responsibly.

GRILLED FISH TACOS with Smoky Lime Crema & Spicy Slaw

 IF you're at a ballgame in San Diego, you just might spot more fish tacos than hot dogs in the stands. America was first introduced to this south-of-the-border creation by Baja surfers, and it quickly became the go-to meal for hungry beachgoers throughout Southern California.

1 Build a charcoal fire for direct grilling using Kingsford® Charcoal and preheat to 450 degrees Fahrenheit. Lightly oil the grates to prevent sticking.

2 Whisk together the crema or sour cream, 1/2 teaspoon smoked paprika, 1 tablespoon of lime juice and zest. Season to taste with salt and pepper; set aside.

3 To make the slaw, toss the coleslaw mix or cabbage with the jalapeño pepper, 2 tablespoons of the olive oil and 2 tablespoons of lime juice. Season to taste with salt and plenty of pepper, adding more lime juice if desired.

4 Rub the fish with the remaining 2 tablespoons of olive oil, and season well with salt, pepper and the remaining smoked paprika. Place the fish onto the grill, flesh side down.

5 Grill for 4 minutes on the first side; then flip and cook for another minute. For your safety, please reference the USDA safe cooking temperatures.

6 Remove from the grill and let rest for five minutes. Flake with a fork. While the fish is resting, grill the tortillas over direct heat until they are warmed, about 30 seconds.

7 To assemble, divide fish among the tortillas, and top with slaw and diced avocado. Drizzle with crema, and top with cilantro, if desired. Serve immediately.

½	cup Mexican crema or sour cream
1 ½	teaspoons smoked paprika, divided
1	tablespoon lime zest
3	tablespoons fresh lime juice
	Kosher salt and ground black pepper, to taste
3	cups coleslaw mix or shredded green cabbage
½	jalapeño pepper, seeded and minced
¼	cup olive oil
1	pound white flaky fish, such as mahi mahi
8	corn or flour tortillas
	Diced avocado, for garnish
	Minced cilantro, for garnish (optional)

MAKES
8
tacos

PREP TIME
20
minutes

COOK TIME
5–6
minutes

GRILLED VEGETABLE FLATBREADS *with Ricotta and Salsa Verde*

The San Francisco Bay Area represents a colorful mosaic of diverse cultures, lifestyles and flavors. Our grilled vegetable flatbread is inspired by the city's strong Italian food heritage, but also features a brilliant salsa verde that takes this non-traditional pizza over the top.

1 To make the salsa verde in a food processor or blender, combine all herbs, lemon zest, 2 teaspoons lemon juice, garlic, capers, anchovy (if using) and red pepper flakes. Process until leaves are finely minced. With machine running, slowly add 1/2 cup olive oil until sauce is a creamy yellow-green color. Salt and pepper to taste.

2 Build a two-zone fire, placing preheated Kingsford® Charcoal briquets on one half of the bottom grill grate and leaving the other side void.

3 Toss zucchini, asparagus and red onions (can substitute 1½–2 pounds seasonal vegetables of choice) with 3 tablespoons olive oil, 3/4 teaspoon salt and 1/4 teaspoon pepper.

4 Grill over direct heat, turning often, until tender and charred in spots, about 5 minutes; transfer to the void side of the grill.

5 Lightly oil grill grate and divide pizza dough in half. Gently roll and stretch each piece into a rectangle or oval about 14x8 inches and transfer to two lightly oiled baking sheets. (If it springs back, cover and let rest 10 minutes, then stretch again).

6 Transfer dough to grill over direct heat. Cook until first side is lightly charred and dough is dry and stiff; one to two minutes. Turn and cook just until reverse side has a few light grill marks; 30 to 60 seconds. Transfer to baking sheets and let cool slightly.

7 Top charred side of dough with the grilled vegetables, dividing evenly. Dollop ricotta over the vegetables on both flatbreads and drizzle with the salsa verde.

8 Cut each flatbread into three to four pieces and serve immediately.

MAKES	PREP TIME	COOK TIME
6-8 servings	**20** minutes	**20** minutes

½	cup parsley leaves and thin stems, lightly packed
¼	cup fresh basil, lightly packed
¼	cup fresh tarragon, lightly packed
¼	cup fresh chives, lightly packed
1	tablespoon lemon zest
2	tablespoons fresh lemon juice
1	garlic clove, smashed
1½	tablespoons capers, rinsed and drained
2	anchovy fillets (optional)
1 to 2	pinches red pepper flakes, or more to taste
¾	cup olive oil, plus more for brushing flatbread
	Kosher salt and freshly ground black pepper, to taste
2	zucchini, sliced diagonally ⅓-inch thick
½	pound asparagus spears, tough ends snapped off
1	red onion, sliced ⅓-inch thick
1	pound ball fresh or frozen pizza dough, thawed
1	cup (8 ounces) ricotta cheese

Index

'Cued Kielbasa Sandwich, 30

Barbecued Baked Potato w/Smoked Pork Shoulder, 42

Bases Loaded Sandwiches: Bacon, Baloney & Brisket, 48

Beer & Cheese Sauced Brats, 78

Burnt Ends Cheesesteak, 64

Byung-Hyun Kim, 84

Cheesesteak Burgers w/ Fries & Coleslaw, 80

Chicago-Style Char Dog, 74

Coal Fired Chicken Arepas, 58

David Ortiz, 10

Dominican Tostones Sliders, 12

Eric Karros, 24

Filet Steak Sandwich, 62

Greek Lamb Burgers w/Tzatziki Sauce, 26

Grilled Boston Lobster Rolls, 16

Grilled Chicken Souvlaki Skewers w/Chopped Greek Salad, 66

Grilled Cuban Sandwiches, 18

Grilled Fish Tacos w/Smoky Lime Crema & Spicy Slaw, 92

Grilled German Goetta Burgers, 76

Grilled Rocky Mountain Oyster Po'Boy, 90

Grilled Tomahawk Pork Chops w/Peach Bourbon Glaze, 60

Grilled Vegetable Flatbreads w/Ricotta & Salsa Verde, 94

Grilled Walleye Sandwiches, 34

Harold Reynolds, 70

Loaded Pork Sausage Sandwiches, 28

Omar Vizquel, 56

Original Nor-Cal BBQ Tri-Tip, 44

Pit Beef Sandwiches, 14

Pulled Pork Poutine, 20

Saucy Buffalo Pig Wings, 32

Smoked Oysters w/Spicy Miso Butter, 46

Smoky Rattlesnake Chili, 88

Spicy Korean-Style Chicken Wings, 86

Tex-Mex Shrimp Cocktail, 40

Vinny Castilla, 38